AROUND THE UNIVERSE IN 80 MAZES

Andy Peters

ARCTURUS

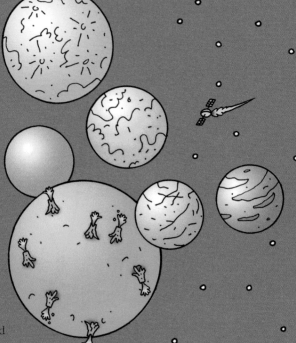

Arcturus

This edition published in 2012 by Arcturus Publishing Limited
26/27 Bickels Yard, 151–153 Bermondsey Street,
London SE1 3HA

ISBN: 978-1-84858-449-5
CH002166EN
Supplier 16, Date 0612, Print Run 1563

Illustrations and mazes designed by Andy Peters
Written by Samantha Noonan
Edited by Kate Overy
Designed by Linda Storey

Printed in Singapore

CONTENTS

Chapter 1
OUT OF THIS WORLD!

Look out for Ted the ginger cat. He's tagged along and pops up in every maze!

Max, Millie and Mojo are camping out in the country for a few nights. All is quiet and still, but the weirdest things can happen when you least expect them…

Follow That Star!

The gang are relaxing under the stars and spotting constellations.
Can you find the way through to the single, bright star?

DID YOU SPOT?

A shooting star

A nosy bat

3 glow worms

Mystery Craft

At dawn, the gang are awakened by a fleet of flying saucers!
Can you direct this bright spaceship to the landing spot?

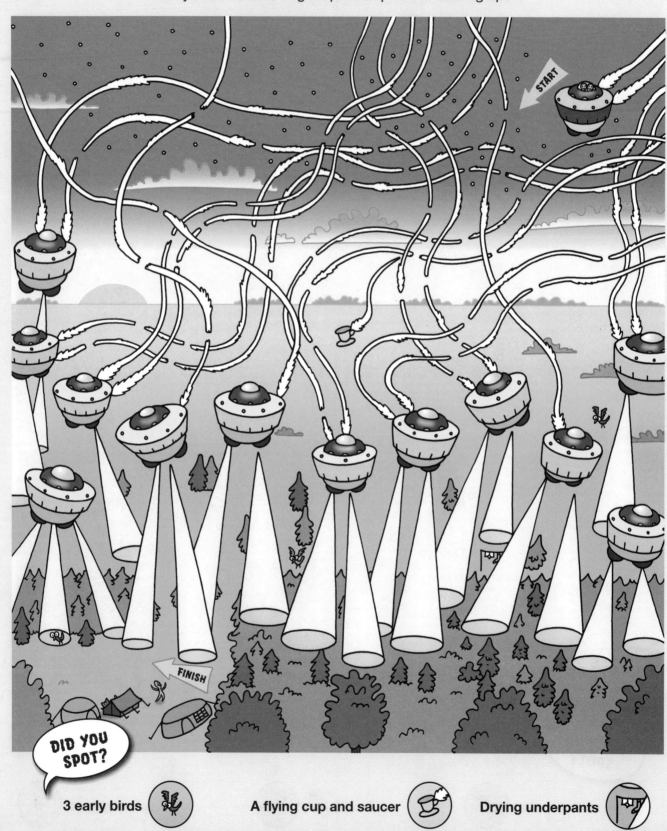

START

FINISH

DID YOU SPOT?

3 early birds

A flying cup and saucer

Drying underpants

Strange Signs

Later that day, Max, Millie and Mojo visit the landing site.
Can you help them find their way through the crop circles?

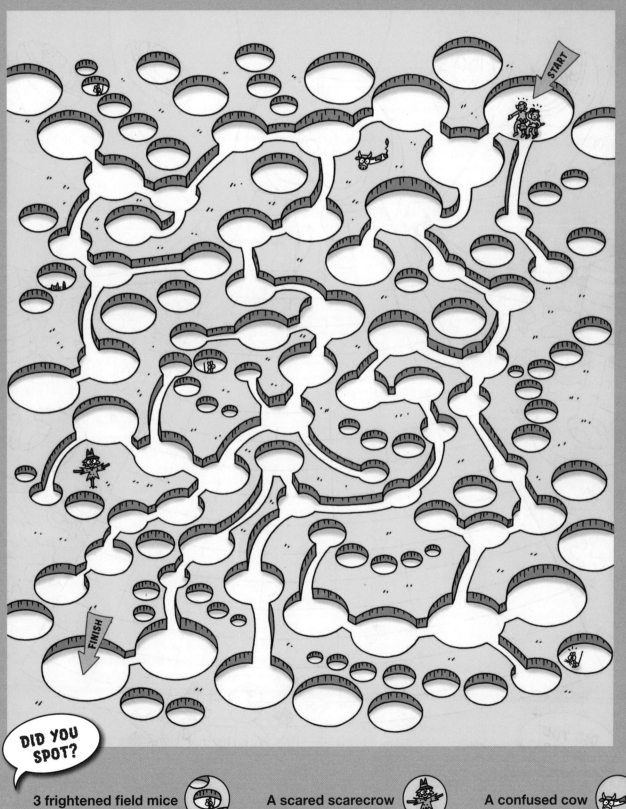

DID YOU SPOT?

3 frightened field mice   A scared scarecrow   A confused cow

Come and Join Us!

An alien has asked Max, Millie and Mojo to join him and his crew
on a very urgent mission. Find the way up the ramp and on to the ship.

3 bewildered bears   The alien captain   The alien dog

Mojo's Dash

Mojo really wants to go on a space adventure with his friends, but he's left his lucky bone behind! Help him rush back to get it before the spaceship takes off.

Ginger Cat Stowaway

Ginger Cat has slipped onto the spaceship too! But he needs to hide away; help him find a dark corner in the engine room.

Space Invaders

The aliens tell Max, Millie and Mojo to come up to the control room of the spaceship to collect their space suits.

DID YOU SPOT?

The space spider   The galactic goldfish   The teddy bear

Alien Welcome

The aliens have thrown a surprise party to welcome the friends on board!

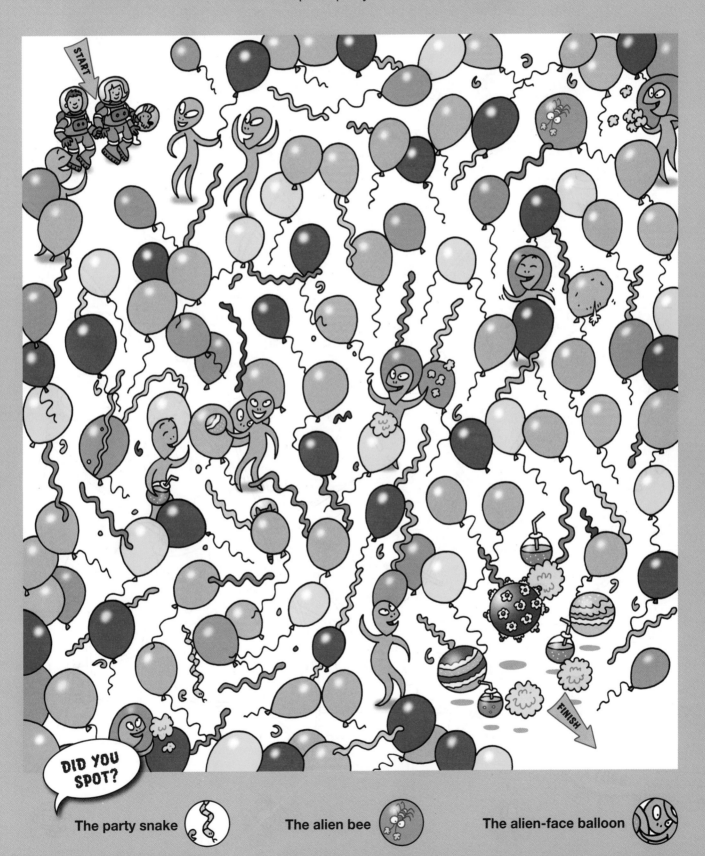

DID YOU SPOT?

The party snake   **The alien bee**   **The alien-face balloon**

Up Through The Atmosphere

It's time to go, but the ship takes off during a meteor shower!
Help steer the spaceship through the meteors and other obstacles.

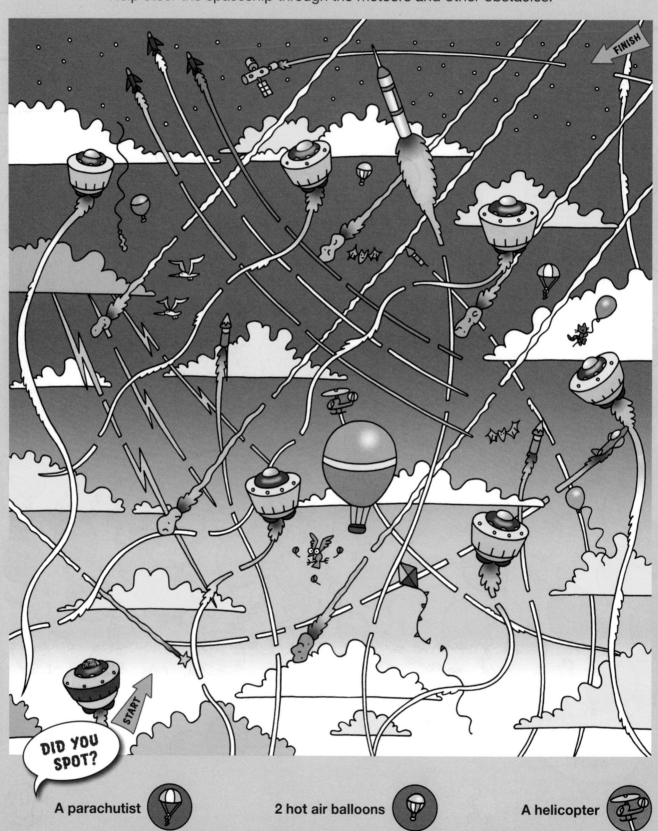

A parachutist   2 hot air balloons   A helicopter

Moon Walk

Max, Millie and Mojo ask if they can take a walk on the moon.
They are very excited to look back at Earth!

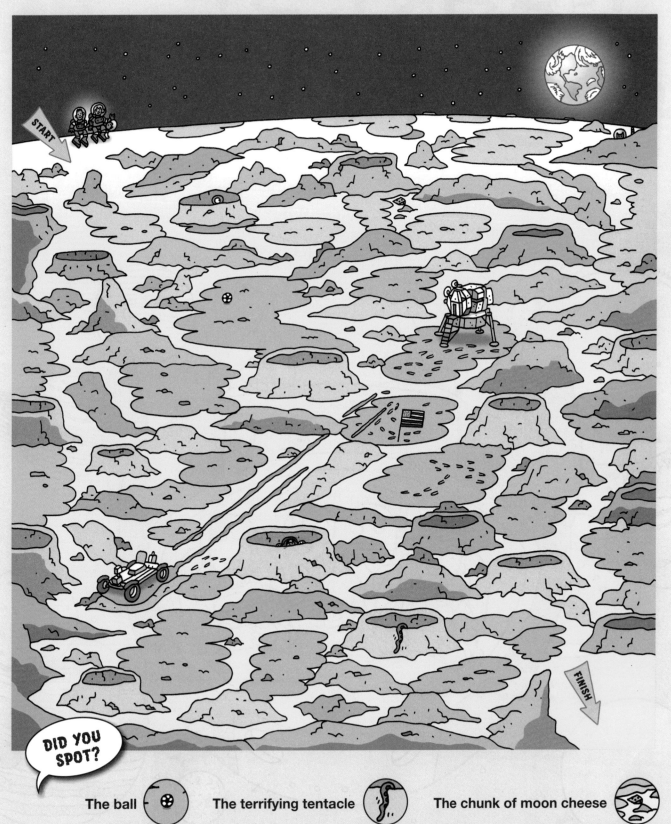

13

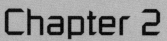

Chapter 2

NEAREST NEIGHBOURS

The aliens explain that the Mother Star, which powers all the other stars in the universe, has been ripped apart and stolen. Without it, all the other stars will die. The aliens have been hunting down all the star pieces and now they just have five left to find.

The Sun

The aliens lend the trio a little space shuttle for searching the planets.
Guide it low to the surface of the Sun so they can look for a star piece.

The toasted marshmallow   **A pair of sunglasses**   **3 sun salamanders**

Magnetic Mercury

Next stop, Mercury! Help the friends fly through the
magnetic field and all the metal objects it is dragging in.

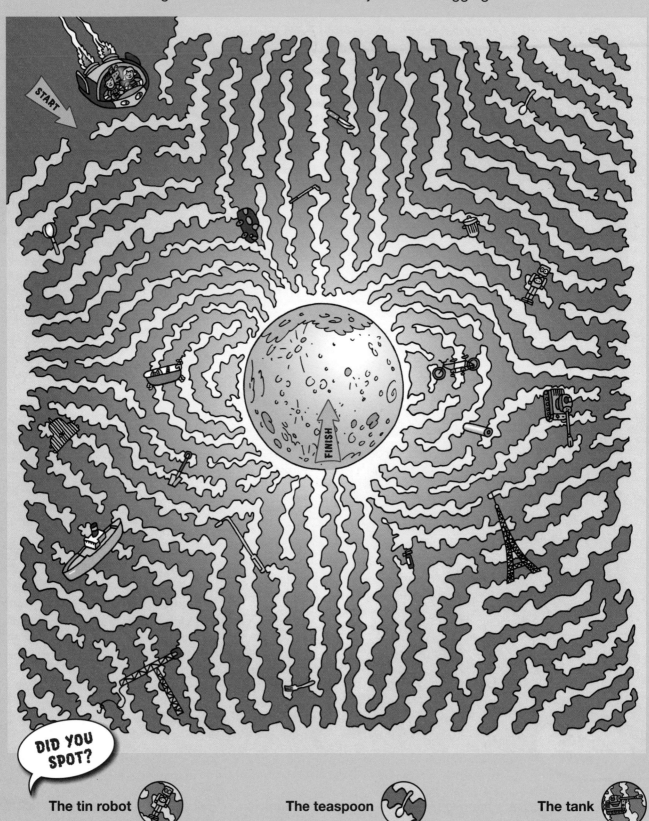

The tin robot

The teaspoon

The tank

Metal Men

The metal men of Mercury have gathered to say hello to the gang,
but the trio have no time to stop! Help them get back to the spaceship.

DID YOU SPOT?

4 lost oil cans   3 loose screws   A remote control

17

Hot Spot

Max, Millie and Mojo have arrived on Venus! Help them find a way around the lava.

The shark fin   The surfing alien   The magma hot tub

Dragon City

The Venusians aren't as friendly as the metal men on Mercury!
Help the gang get through this scary city quickly.

The baby dragon   **The ruby collar**   **The traffic lights**

Star Map

The aliens have asked Max, Millie and Mojo to navigate the way to Mars.
Can you see on the star map which route they should take?

DID YOU SPOT?

A blue star

4 green stars

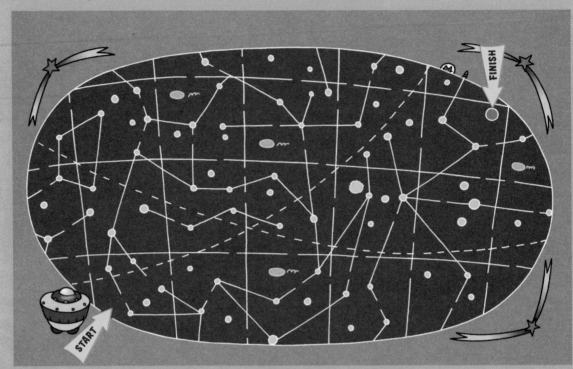

Mojo Lost!

Mojo was having fun exploring the ship, but now he's
lost in the alien canteen! Help him find his way out.

DID YOU SPOT?

The alien
pizza

3 empty
plates

The Red Planet

Max, Millie and Mojo have made it to Mars!
Now they need to search the surface for star pieces.

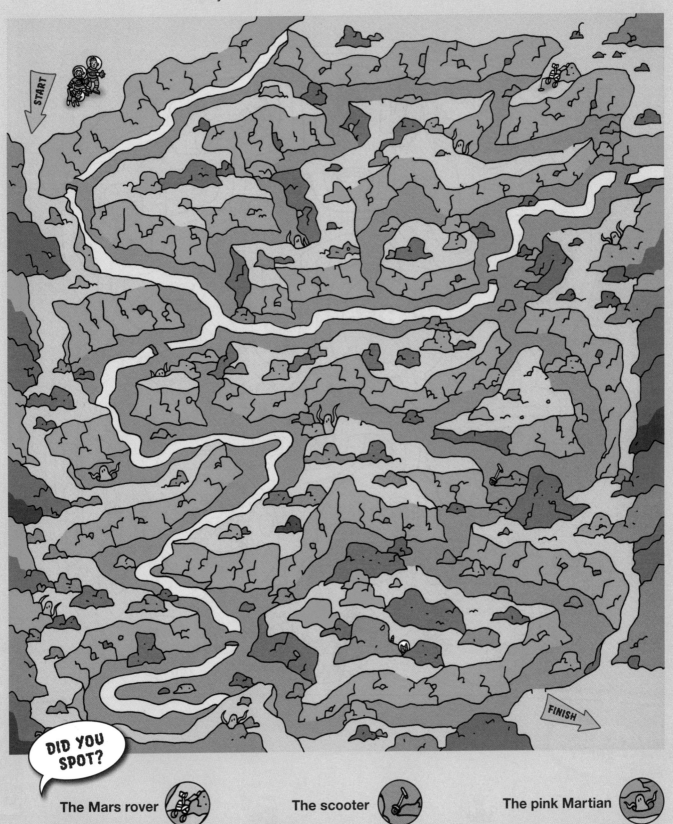

Life on Mars

The aliens decide to stop overnight on Mars, so Max, Millie and Mojo
stay with a Martian family. Help them find their bedroom.

DID YOU SPOT?

The Martian cat   The Martian watching TV   The Martian taking a shower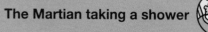

Alien School Time

The friends search everywhere on Mars for star pieces – even in the school!

Chapter 3
DEEP SPACE

The aliens are very grateful to Max, Millie and Mojo for finding the first star piece (did you spot it?) and they fly on to find more. Join the friends as they venture into deep space.

Asteroid Belt

Before they can reach any more planets, our crew need to navigate
the famous asteroid belt – can you get them out in one piece?

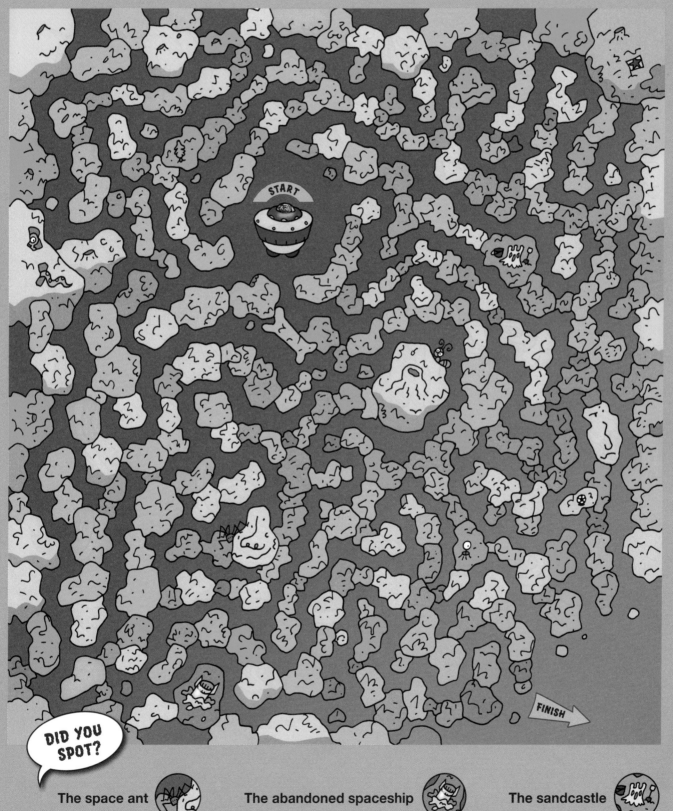

The space ant

The abandoned spaceship

The sandcastle

The Eye of Jupiter

Is there a star piece swirling in the giant storms on Jupiter?
Help Max, Millie and Mojo through the maze.

DID YOU SPOT?

The alien with 3 arms   The balloon   The kite

Many Moons

Did you know that Jupiter has 64 moons? Help steer the friends around them all.

DID YOU SPOT?

Europa the icy moon   Io the volcanic moon   Callisto the ancient moon

The Lord of the Rings

Spacecrafts can easily crash and burn in Saturn's rings.
Guide our friends through safely towards the surface of Saturn.

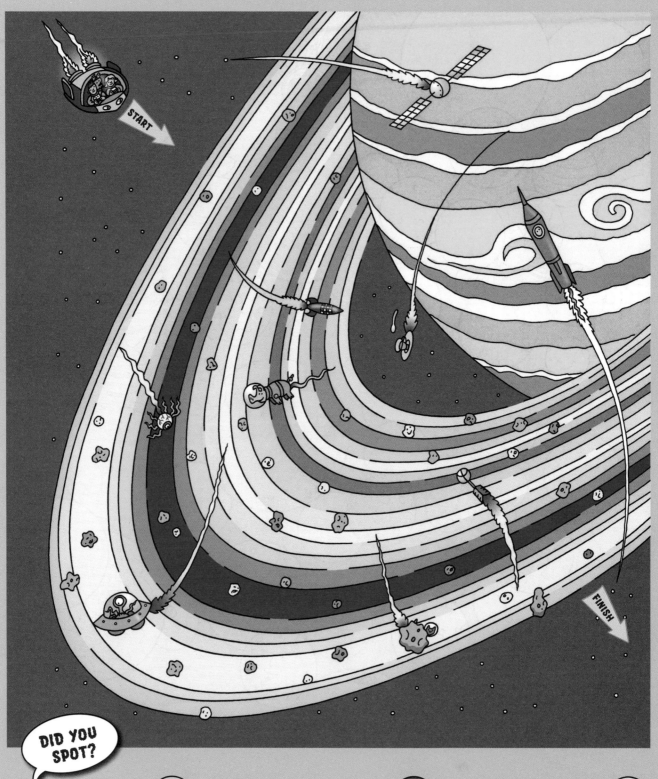

The space pig   The flying cup and saucer   The smiley meteorite

Alien Castle

The gang have been invited to meet the King of Saturn in his giant palace. Help them find the way to the throne room.

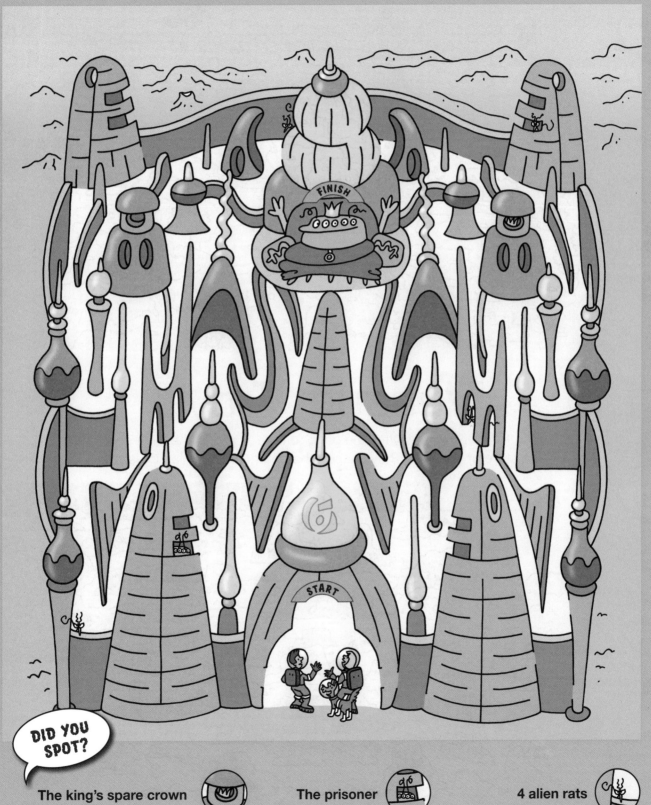

DID YOU SPOT?

The king's spare crown   The prisoner   4 alien rats

Cat Trails

Ginger Cat wasn't fast enough and has lost track of the gang!
Help him through the deadly Saturn swamp to find his friends.

The shopping trolley

The swamp monster

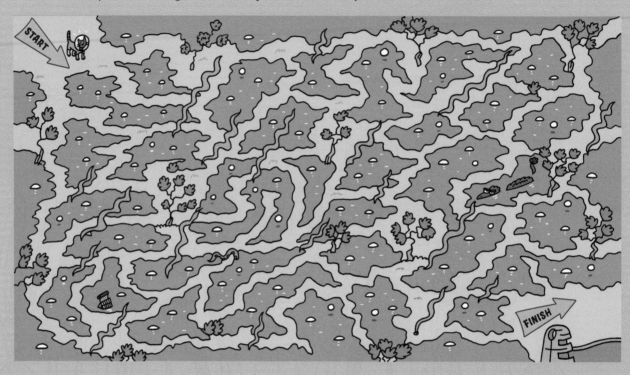

Treasure Trove

The King of Saturn invites the gang to take anything they like from his store of treasure. They choose the beautiful Saturnian Crystals.

A large bag of money

Two golden candlesticks

Stormy Sea

The shuttle switches to underwater mode on Neptune. Can you spot any star pieces?

King Mermartian

King Mermartian's trident

The red star piece

The Uncanny Planet

Uranus is covered in mist and is not a very nice place.
The gang decide to hurry back to the shuttle.

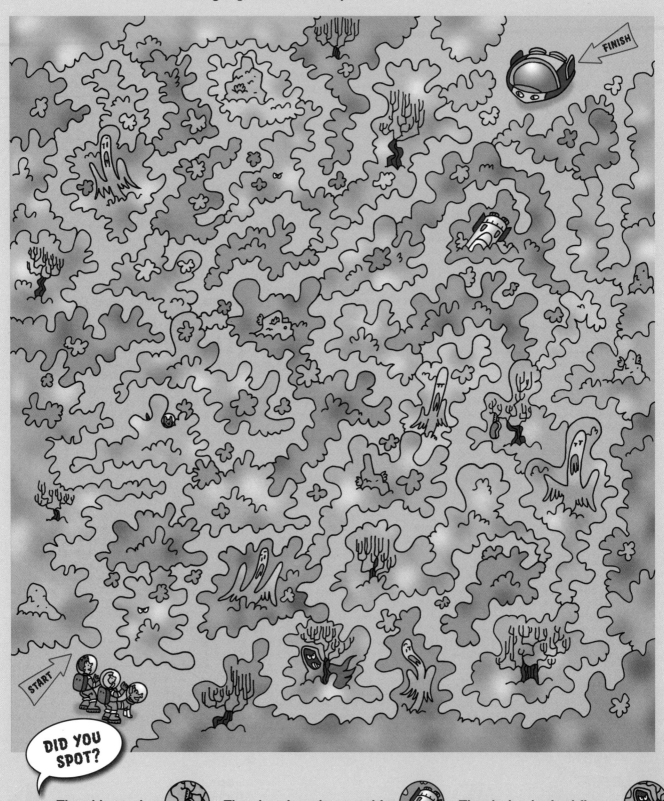

The ski goggles   **The abandoned spaceship**   **The dark, cloaked figure**

Play on Pluto

Our friends have arrived on Pluto, the number one sports venue in the galaxy, and two teams are about to play Spaceball! Help them get to their seats.

DID YOU SPOT?

The pair of green hover boots   The referee   A Venusian

Chapter 4
BEYOND THE MILKY WAY

Max, Millie and Mojo are pleased to have found two star pieces in the solar system but there are still three left to find and the universe is a big place!

Hyperspace

There is no time to lose, so the aliens decide to jump into hyperspace so they can travel at the speed of light! Help them navigate around the stars.

Milky Way

It takes a long time to get out of the Milky Way galaxy and into deep space.
Guide the spaceship through the spiral.

The green nebula **The alien in the space station** **4 shooting stars**

Traffic Jam

Oh no! There is a big traffic jam on the Andromeda Highway!
Guide the shuttle through all the other spaceships.

DID YOU SPOT?

The alien traffic lights   The space police   The parking attendant

Nebula

The friends decide to search a star nursery, where baby stars are born. To get there they have to go right into the middle of a nebula. Can you steer them in?

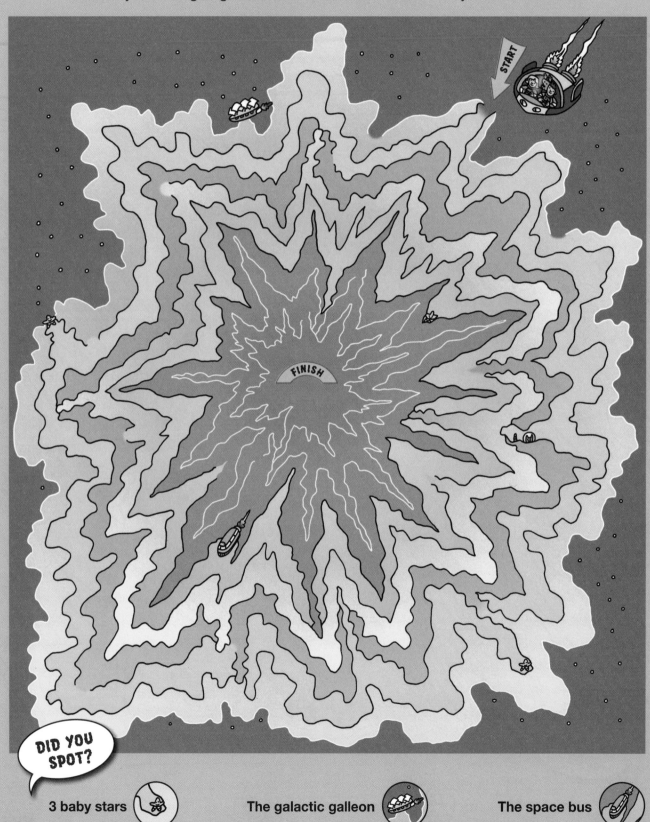

3 baby stars   **The galactic galleon**   **The space bus**

Star Nursery

This is one of the brightest places in the universe, so put your starglasses on!

Alien Drive-In

Next stop, a drive-in space movie! The friends fly around
the audience asking if anyone has news of the star pieces.

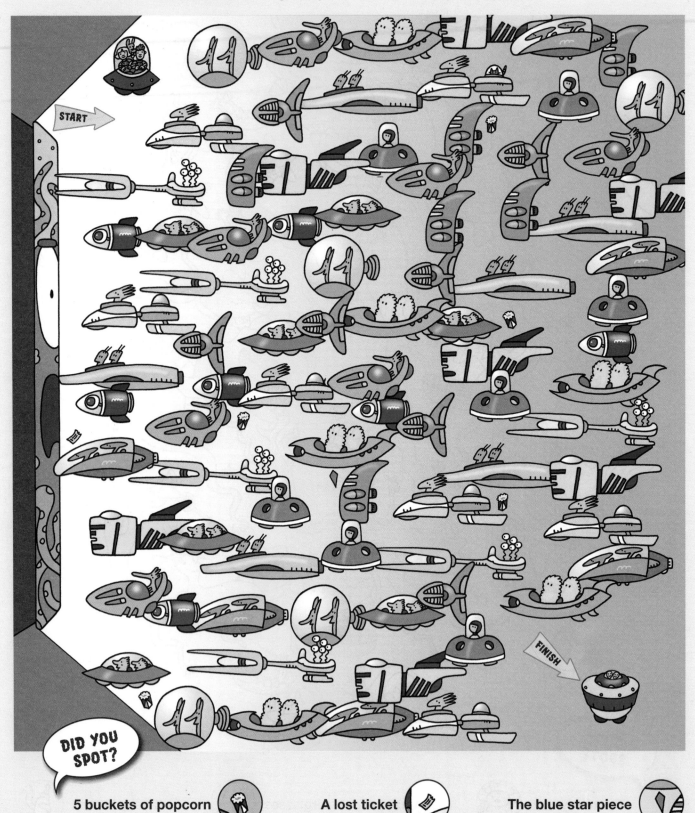

DID YOU SPOT?

5 buckets of popcorn   **A lost ticket**   **The blue star piece**

Spacesick Mojo

All this whizzing around is making Mojo a bit spacesick!
Help him find the way to the medical bay.

The alien with one eye

The alien vending machine

Ginger Shadow

The aliens have noticed something sneaking around their ship and
they are curious. Help them find sneaky Ginger Cat's hiding place.

A cat collar

4 paw prints

41

Theme Park Thrills

An alien amusement park is very different to one back on Earth!
Help Max, Millie and Mojo find a way through.

DID YOU SPOT?

The blue fish   The alien balloon   The pink cotton candy

Alien Supermarket

The aliens are running low on supplies so they stop at the biggest supermarket in the universe! Can you guide them through to the exit?

DID YOU SPOT?

A baby alien   4 purple carrots   The three-eyed shopper

Chapter 5

TIME IS RUNNING OUT!

The aliens can see that some stars are starting to fade. It's urgent that they collect all the star pieces! They have heard that the Zoid aliens from the planet Zosma are the ones who stole the star pieces, so they decide to go there to find them.

Inside the Cruiser

The aliens' little spaceship could not manage the huge journey to Zosma on its own, so they have hitched a lift on an intergalactic Space Cruiser! Max, Millie and Mojo want to go up to the star deck.

DID YOU SPOT?

A Venusian

An arcade game

A purple alien

Giant Spaceport

The cruiser lands at a giant spaceport near Zosma.
Help the gang find their way back to their spaceship.

The alien cat in a box   **The alien with a purple belly**   **The human**

Suspects' Planet

Our friends arrive at the planet Zosma but the Zoids fire so many missiles up at them, they can't land! Help them to dodge the missiles and get away.

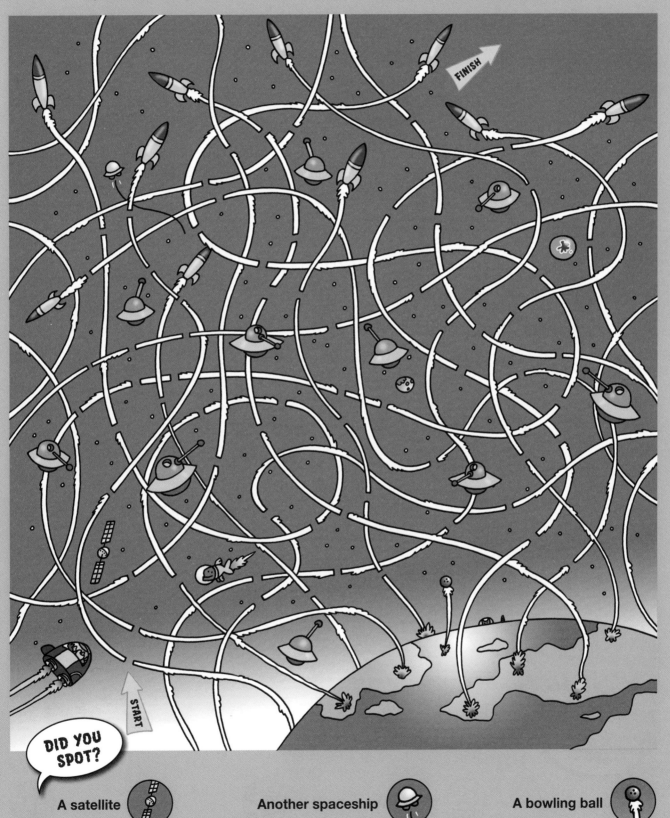

DID YOU SPOT?

A satellite

Another spaceship

A bowling ball

Spacewalk

The ship sustained some damage from the Zoid missiles. Help the gang spacewalk from the hatch to the broken bit to repair it.

Sudden Supernova!

A nearby star suddenly explodes, creating a supernova! Help our friends get away.

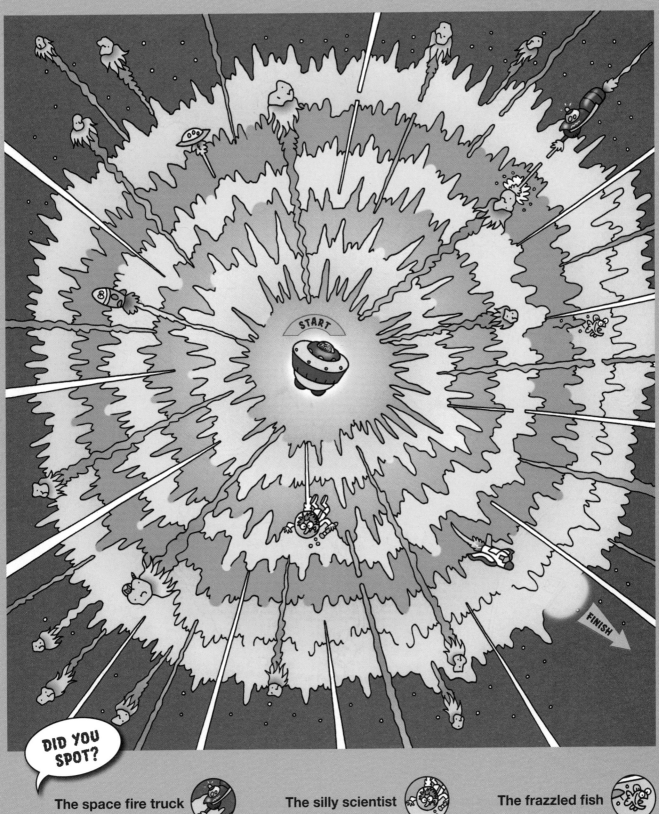

Supermassive Black Hole

The gang couldn't get away fast enough and are being sucked into a supermassive black hole! Help them avoid all the objects being sucked in with them.

The black hole monster **The kitchen sink** **The pizza**

The Edge of the Universe

The black hole has spat our friends out at the very edge
of the universe – an extremely strange place indeed!

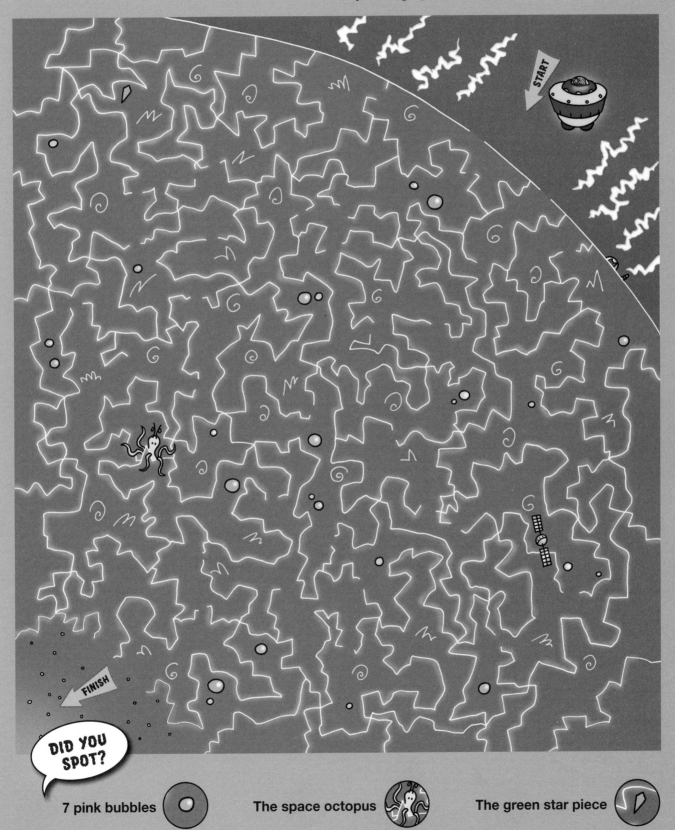

START

FINISH

DID YOU SPOT?

7 pink bubbles   The space octopus   The green star piece

Jungle Planet

The ship is desperate for fuel so the aliens land on a strange planet to find some. Guide Max, Millie and Mojo through the alien jungle.

52

6 alien frogs   **The alien lion**   **The alien banana plants**

Snake Struggle

Ginger Cat has got caught in the coils of a giant space snake! Help him to find his way out.

DID YOU SPOT?

The alien spider

The alien snake eggs

River Rafting

The local aliens tell the gang they must travel to the city to find fuel.
They give them a boat to go down the river.

DID YOU SPOT?

The funny fish

The toy boat

Chapter 6

HELP IS AT HAND

The aliens decide they need to go to the Capital of the universe and ask the ruler, President Zendergast, to help them find the last star piece.

Wormhole

The fastest way to the Capital is through a wormhole, but watch out for space worms!

Which Way?

The inside of a wormhole can be a confusing place! Make sure our heroes go the right way.

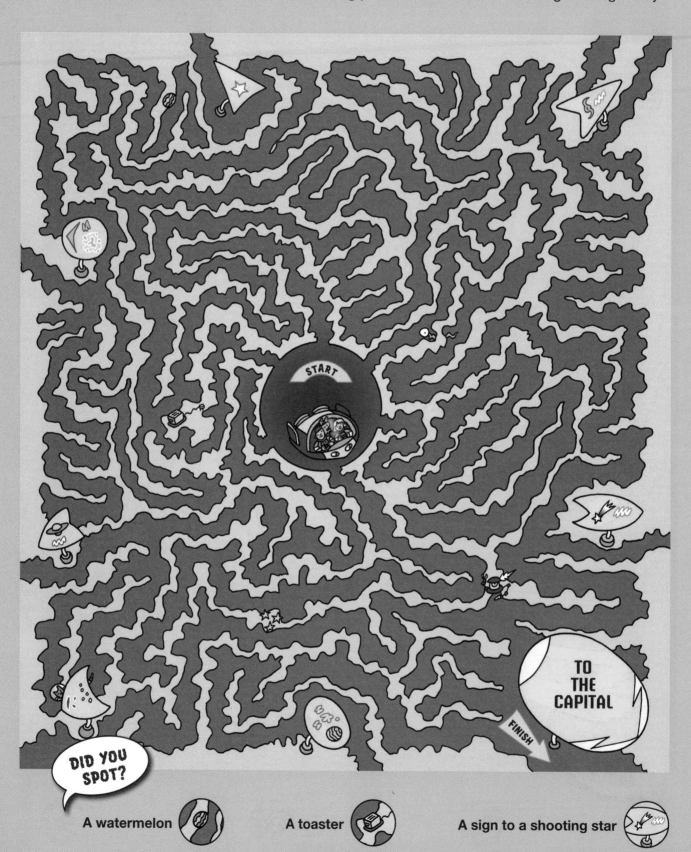

56 A watermelon A toaster A sign to a shooting star

The Capital of the Universe

The friends have arrived at the Capital! But they need to pass through
all the checkpoints before they are allowed to approach the planet.

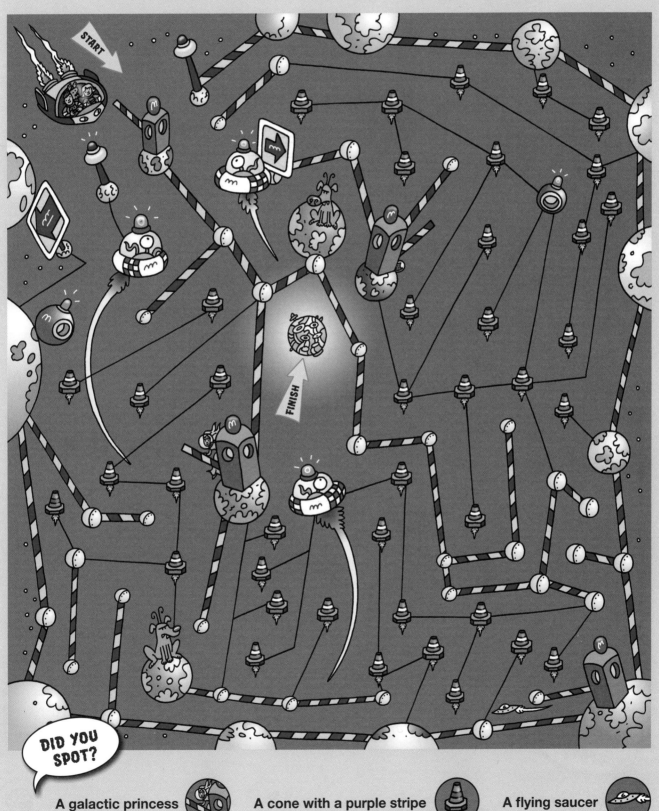

DID YOU SPOT?

A galactic princess   A cone with a purple stripe   A flying saucer

On the Ground

Max, Millie and Mojo would love to take in all the strange sights, but they must hurry along the space roads to see President Zendergast.

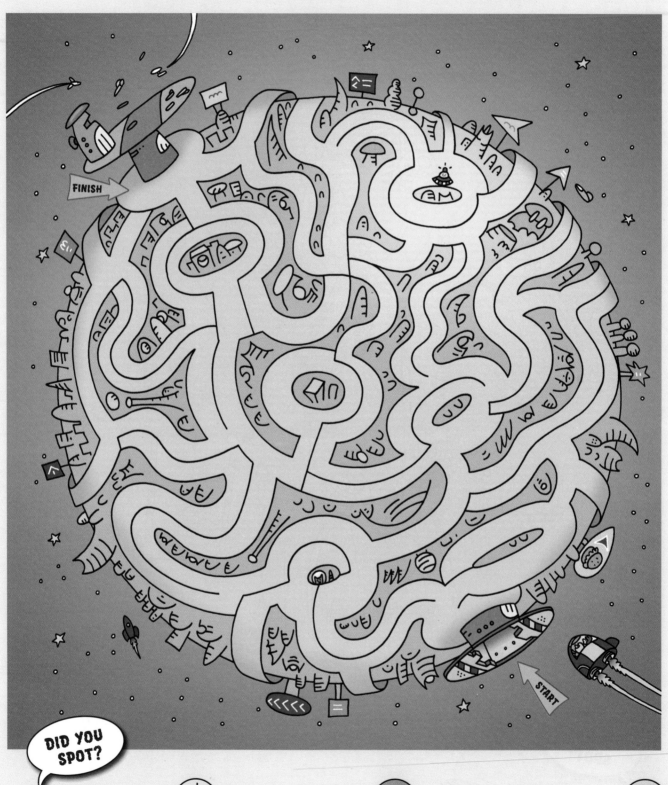

Alien Library

The gang take a shortcut through a giant library. Shh!

DID YOU SPOT?

5 'Shh' signs   The Guides to Earth section   The alien cat napping

Stomach Rumble

Mojo is very hungry. He didn't like the alien food offered on the ship, and now he can smell something like Earth sausages!

DID YOU SPOT?

An alien bird

A hover frisbee

Bare Paws!

Oh no, Ginger Cat has left his space boots behind after taking a nap!
Help him retrace his steps to get them.

DID YOU SPOT?

A sinking toy boat

An alien duck

Tall Tower

At last, the friends have made it to the tower where President Zendergast lives.
Find a way to the top.

Queue Jump!

There are hundreds of people waiting to talk to the President so our friends have to dash around the barriers and jump the queue before it's too late!

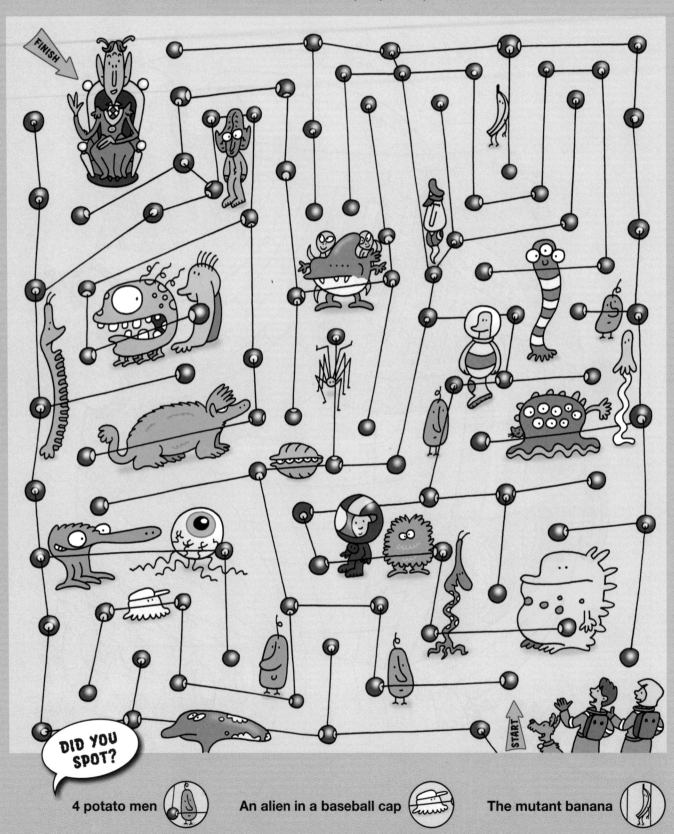

4 potato men   **An alien in a baseball cap**   **The mutant banana**

Jet Chase

Through the window of the President's tower, the gang spot a Zoid flying away with the final star piece! They put on jet packs to give chase to him.

DID YOU SPOT?

3 beautiful butterflies   A bewildered bat   A broken biplane

Chapter 7
THIS MEANS WAR!

Max, Millie and Mojo couldn't catch up with the crafty Zoid. But he's sent a message challenging our heroes to a battle for the final star piece. They need to find some friends to help them defeat the Zoids once and for all!

The Lazons

The Lazon aliens make the best laser guns in the universe and agree to help fight the Zoids. Help Max, Millie and Mojo safely through the laser beams.

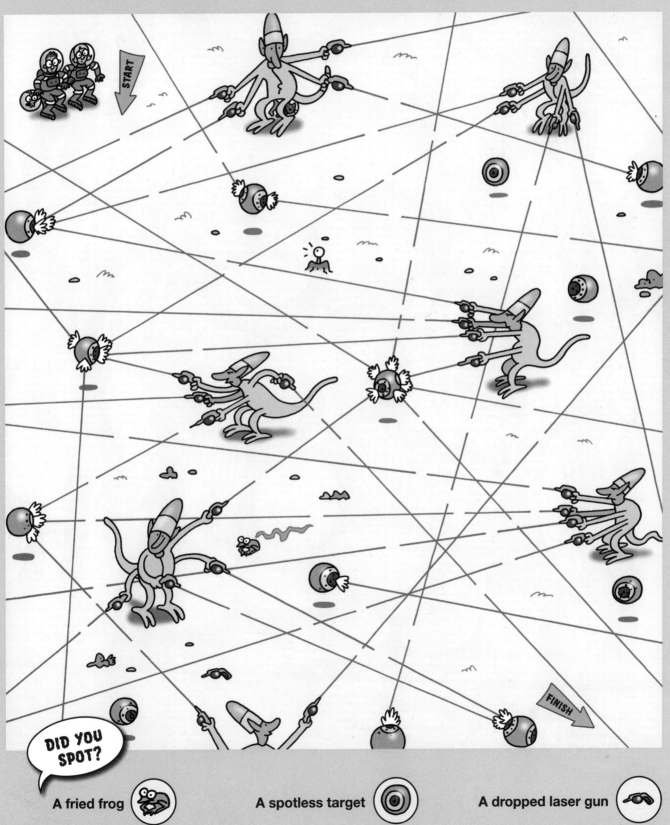

DID YOU SPOT?

A fried frog   A spotless target   A dropped laser gun

Intergalactic Travels

The gang needs to whizz around the galaxies to find more people to help them!

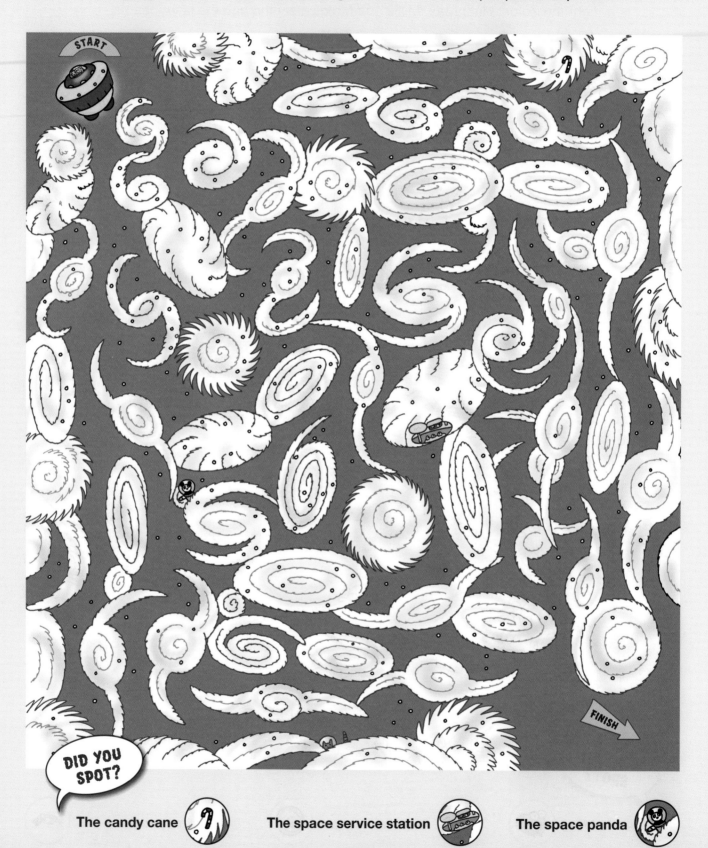

The candy cane   **The space service station**   **The space panda**

Frozen Planet

The gang arrive on a planet of ice and snow inhabited by the Wubbles.
Help them find a route to the Wubble mayor to ask for help.

DID YOU SPOT?

The Wubble fishing

A white-bellied Wubble

The yeti footprint

Star Surfers

Next, the gang try to recruit the star surfers who hang out near the Orion Nebula.

3 space jellyfish   **The star helmet**   **The green surfboard**

Squid Planet

The gang have a limited air supply so they can't spend long underwater on Planet Squid.
Help them find the leader quickly!

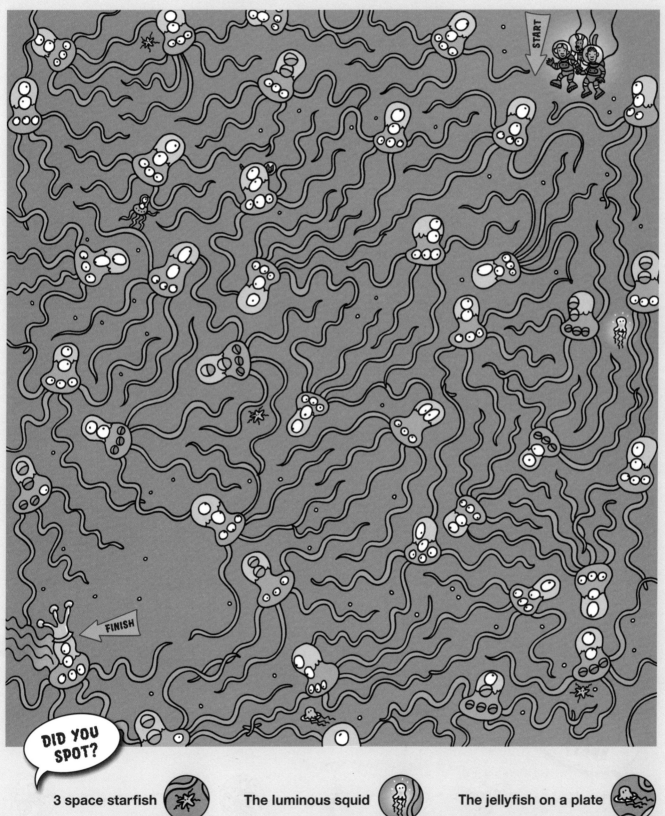

DID YOU SPOT?

3 space starfish   The luminous squid   The jellyfish on a plate

Crab Nebula

The clicky crabs of the Crab Nebula promise that they will help in the battle.

The blue crab   **The hermit crab**   **King Crab**

Neutron Star

Our friends need to get some ammunition for the battle. Help them collect one of the most explosive things in the universe – the core of a neutron star.

START

FINISH

DID YOU SPOT?

3 horseshoe magnets

A red rocket

A box of matches

Mojo the Mechanic

Mojo is the only one small enough to wriggle through the engine and put the neutron star piece in the firing tube.

DID YOU SPOT?

A tool box

3 bolts

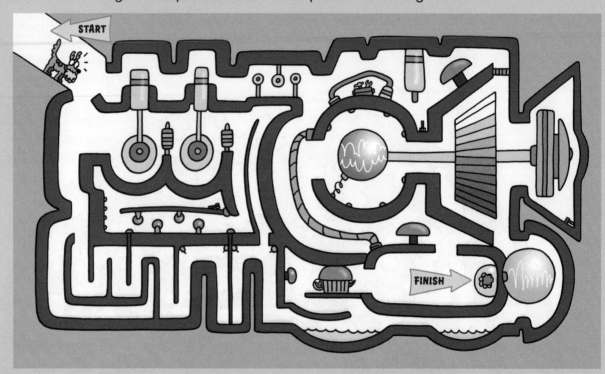

Army Formation

When the gang arrive at the battle arena, everyone else is already there! Steer the shuttle to the front.

DID YOU SPOT?

Soldier Spider

Combat Duck

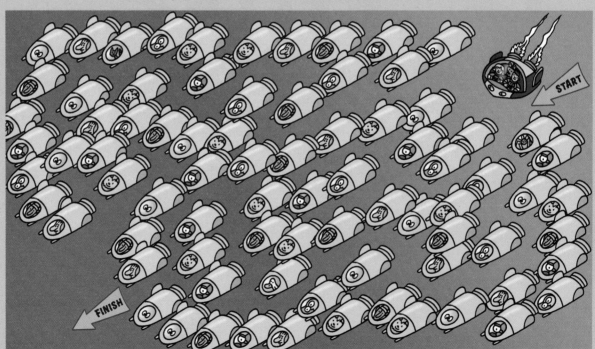

Star Quest

While everyone is distracted by the battle, Max, Millie and Mojo
steer their shuttle to the Zoid's base to steal back the last star piece!

The yellow star piece   **A ball**   **An alien ejecting**

Chapter 8

SAVING THE UNIVERSE

Hooray! Max, Millie and Mojo have got the final star piece. Now all they need to do is put the Mother Star back together.

Garbage Dump

Max, Millie and Mojo are on their way back with the star piece to meet the aliens when they take a wrong turn and end up at an alien garbage dump!

DID YOU SPOT?

3 alien dump dwellers   The waste collector   A dumped diamond

Turn on the Lights

The gang need to attach their star pieces and then light the flame at the core of the Mother Star. They've nearly done it!

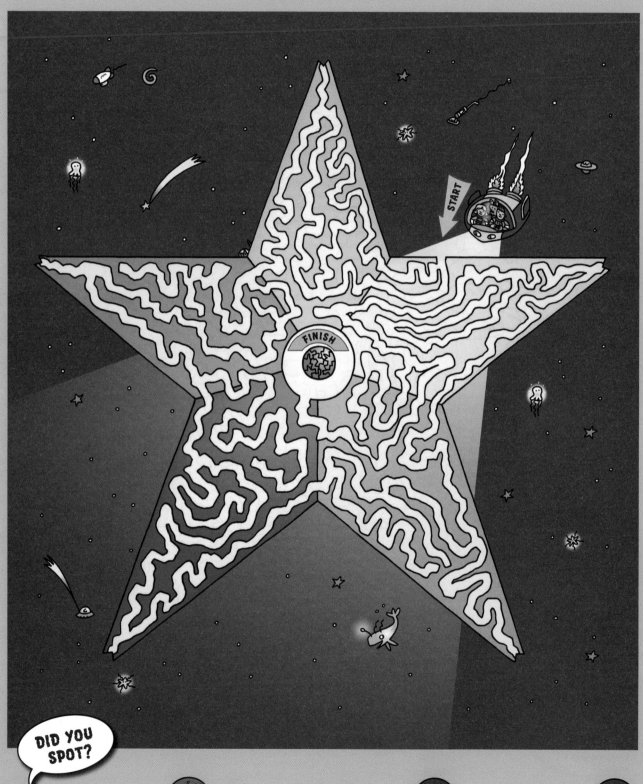

Space angler fish

Space vacuum cleaner

Space blimp

Hungry Heroes

President Zendergast throws a banquet in honour of Max, Millie and Mojo to say thank you for saving the universe. And best of all, he gives Max and Millie a baby star each to take home!

2 aliens with 5 eyes   **Alien cakes**   **The alien drink**

Galactic Gift

Max, Millie and Mojo are taken to the best spaceship factory in the universe where they are given their very own spaceship!

A ghost in the machine The factory boss 5 star-shaped screws

Journey Home

It is time for the trio to fly themselves home in their brand new spaceship. All their friends come out to say goodbye.

DID YOU SPOT?

The alien in a balloon   **A baseball cap**   **A Wubble head balloon**

Blue Planet

The friends need to make sure they land in the right place – Earth is a big planet!
Guide them to their destination.

DID YOU SPOT?

A satellite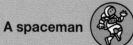

A spaceman

A green alien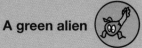

Big Cat Jump

Ginger Cat has decided to parachute home. Help him to land safely.

Dizzy Mojo

Mojo feels very dizzy after all that space travel! Help him to navigate his way out of the spaceship.

Home Sweet Home

The friends are very glad to be back on Earth, but they
need to collect their tent before they can go home.

START

FINISH

DID YOU
SPOT?

A little rabbit

A spaceship spotter

2 baby stars

Shooting Stars

It's time for the baby stars to go to their new home in the sky above Max, Millie and Mojo's house.
One has already made it, but can you help the other one through the fireworks?

DID YOU SPOT?

A star nurse   A rainbow firework   A wise old owl

Answers

Follow That Star!

page 5

Strange Signs

page 7

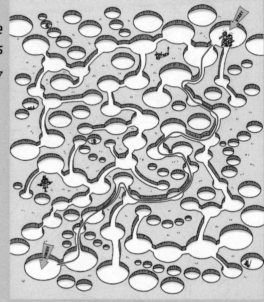

Mystery Craft

page 6

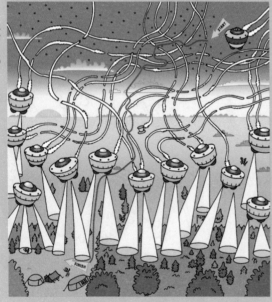

Come and Join Us

page 8

Mojo's Dash
page 9

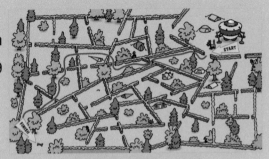

Alien Welcome
page 11

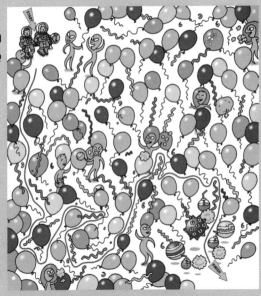

Ginger Cat Stowaway
page 9

Up Through The Atmosphere
page 12

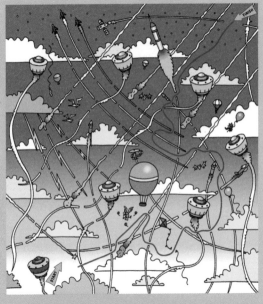

Space Invaders
page 10

Moon Walk
page 13

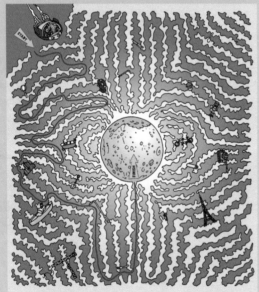

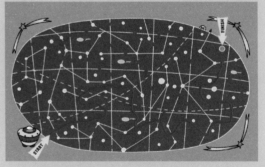

The Red
Planet
page 21

Asteroid Belt

page 25

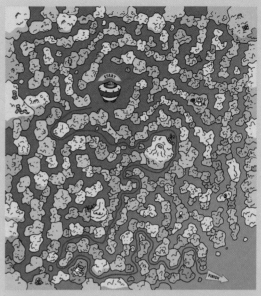

Life on Mars
page 22

The Eye of
Jupiter

page 26

Alien
Schooltime

page 23

**The pink
star piece**

Many Moons

page 27

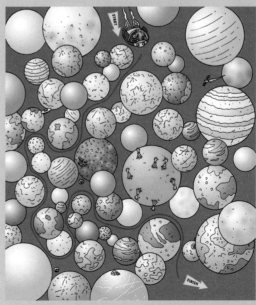

The Lord of
the Rings
page 28

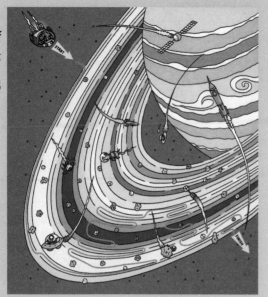

Treasure
Trove
page 30

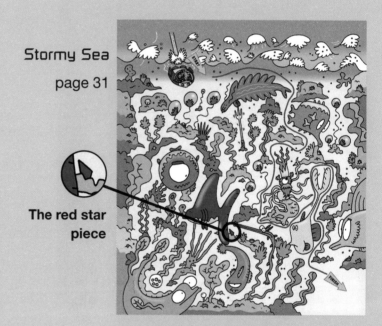

Alien Castle
page 29

Stormy Sea
page 31

**The red star
piece**

The Uncanny
Planet
page 32

Cat Trails
page 30

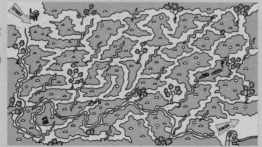

Play on Pluto
page 33

Traffic Jam
page 37

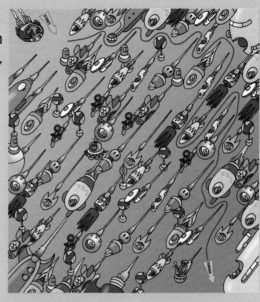

Hyperspace
page 35

Nebula
page 38

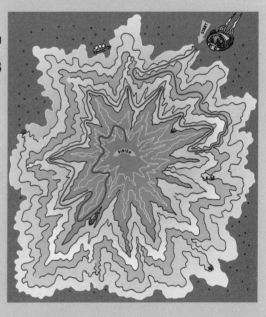

Milky Way
page 36

Star Nursery
page 39

Alien Drive-In
page 40

The blue star piece

Spacesick Mojo
page 41

Ginger Shadow
page 41

Theme Park Thrills
page 42

Alien Supermarket
page 43

Inside the Cruiser
page 45

Giant Spaceport
page 46

Suspects'
Planet

page 47

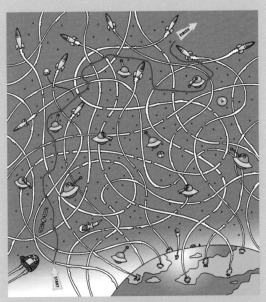

Supermassive
Black Hole

page 50

Spacewalk

page 48

The Edge of
the Universe

page 51

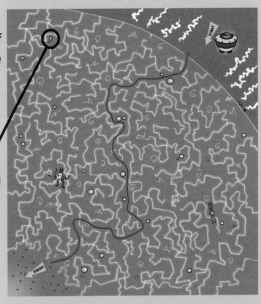

**The green
star piece**

Sudden
Supernova!

page 49

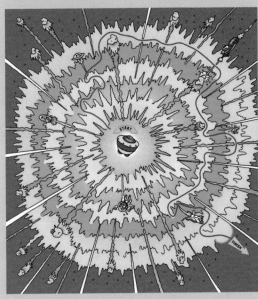

Jungle Planet

page 52

Snake
Struggle

page 53

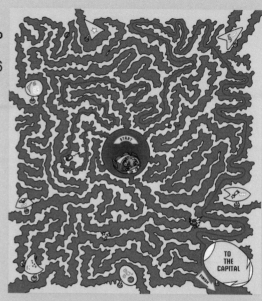

Which Way?

page 56

River Rafting

page 53

The Capital of
the Universe

page 57

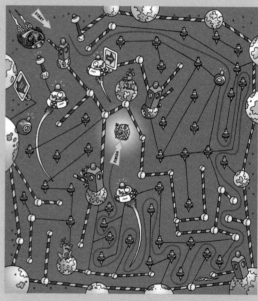

Wormhole

page 55

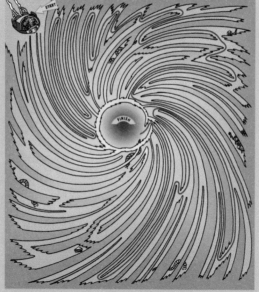

On the
Ground

page 58

Alien Library

page 59

Queue Jump!

page 62

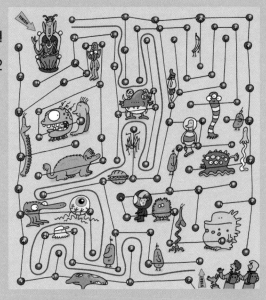

Tummy Rumble

page 60

Jet Chase

page 63

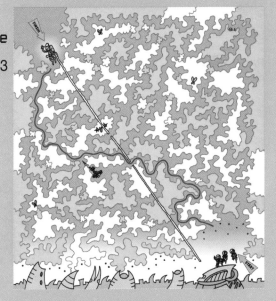

Bare Paws!

page 60

Tall Tower

page 61

The Lazons

page 65

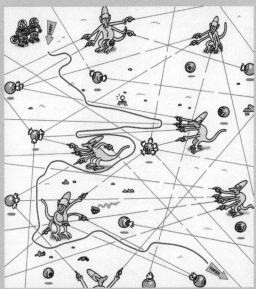

Intergalactic
Travels
page 66

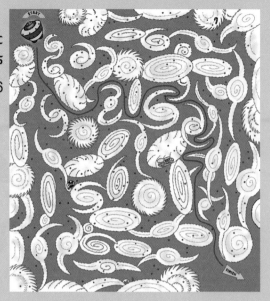

Squid Planet
page 69

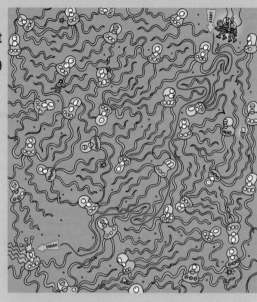

Frozen Planet
page 67

Crab Nebula
page 70

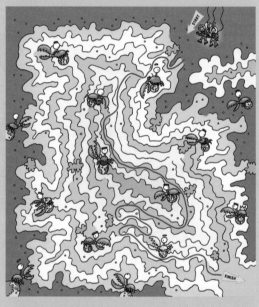

Star Surfers
page 68

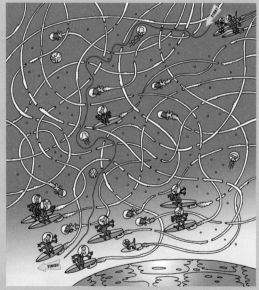

Neutron Star
page 71

Mojo the
Mechanic

page 72

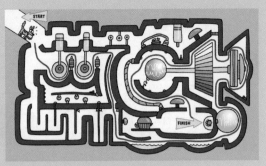

Garbage
Dump

page 75

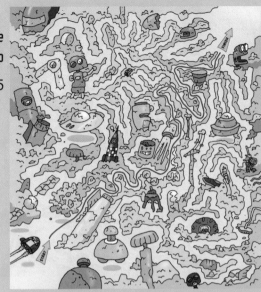

Army
Formation

page 72

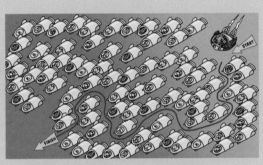

Turn on
the Lights

page 76

Star Quest

page 73

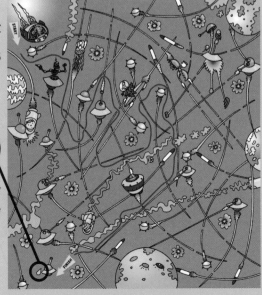

**The yellow
star piece**

Hungry
Heroes

page 77

Galactic Gift
page 78

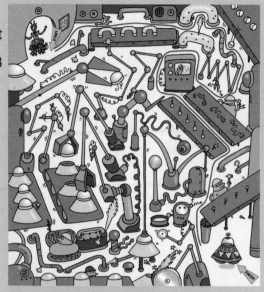

Big Cat Jump
page 81

Dizzy Mojo
page 81

Journey Home
page 79

Home Sweet Home
page 82

Blue Planet
page 80

Shooting Stars
page 83